How to Sparkle at
Grammar and Punctuation

Irene Yates

Brilliant
PUBLICATIONS

We hope you and your class enjoy using this book. Other books in the series include:

Maths titles
How to Sparkle at Addition and Subtraction to 20   978 1 897675 28 1
How to Sparkle at Counting to 10   978 1 897675 27 4
How to Sparkle at Beginning Multiplication and Division   978 1 897675 30 4
How to Sparkle at Maths Fun   978 1 897675 86 1
How to Sparkle at Number Bonds   978 1 897675 34 2

Science titles
How to Sparkle at Assessing Science   978 1 897675 20 5
How to Sparkle at Science Investigations   978 1 897675 36 6

English titles
How to Sparkle at Alphabet Skills   978 1 897675 17 5
How to Sparkle at Grammar and Punctuation   978 1 897675 19 9
How to Sparkle at Nursery Rhymes   978 1 897675 16 8
How to Sparkle at Phonics   978 1 897675 14 4
How to Sparkle at Prediction Skills   978 1 897675 15 1
How to Sparkle at Word Level Activities   978 1 897675 90 8
How to Sparkle at Writing Stories and Poems   978 1 897675 18 2
How to Sparkle at Reading Comprehension   978 1 903853 44 3

Festive title
How to Sparkle at Christmas Time   978 1 897675 62 5

To find out more details on any of our resources, please log onto our website: www.brilliantpublications.co.uk.

Published by Brilliant Publications
Unit 10, Sparrow Hall Farm, Edlesborough, Dunstable, Bedfordshire, LU6 2ES, UK

E-mail: info@brilliantpublications.co.uk
Website: www.brilliantpublications.co.uk

General information enquiries:
Tel: 01525 222292

The name Brilliant Publications and the logo are registered trademarks.

Written by Irene Yates
Illustrated by Kate Ford
Cover illustration by Sue Woollatt

Printed in the UK.
First published in 1997. Reprinted 1998.
10 9 8 7 6 5 4 3 2

© Irene Yates 1997
Printed ISBN 978 1 897675 19 9
ebbok ISBN   978 0 85747 060 7

Contents

	Page		Page
Introduction	4	Finish the sentence	26
How to use this book	5	Start the sentence	27
Links to the National Curriculum	6	Sentences	28
Extension ideas	7	Capitals and full stops	29
		What's wrong?	30
Doing words	8	Right order	31
Naming things	9	Secret code	32
Choose the right word	10	Missing words	33
Word puzzle	11	Gingerbread man	34
People's names	12	In the box	35
-ing words	13	In the circle	36
Describing words	14	Lots of lists	37
Describe yourself	15	Capital letters	38
Making pairs	16	Don't forget the capital letter	39
Opposites	17	Places have names	40
Get the right order	18	Surprise! surprise!	41
Good order	19	Questions, questions	42
Thinking of words	20	Question quiz	43
Missing verbs	21	Get the right order	44
Think of a word	22	The alphabet	45
Think of an opposite	23	Noun wordsearch	46
Beginning sounds	24	Adjective wordsearch	47
Sentence sense	25	Verb wordsearch	48

Introduction

How to Sparkle at Grammar and Punctuation contains 41 photocopiable ideas for use with 5-7 year olds. The book provides a flexible, but structured, resource for teaching children to understand and use parts of speech and punctuation.

In order to develop the ability to write and speak effectively, to their optimum potential, children need to acquire knowledge of good syntax and correct punctuation. Because the concepts are somewhat abstract, they are often quite difficult for children to assimilate. However, this point only proves the case for constant reinforcement. Some children will have to hear the rules of punctuation over and over again before they actually understand them, others seem to have a natural instinct for them. The same goes for grammar.

Some children find it very difficult, because they are in the process of developing their own skills of communication, to step outside the language and be able to discuss it as something that may be looked at, pondered over, deconstructed. Others understand immediately that language is something alive and flowing, something that they may learn about.

One of the most difficult concepts for children to understand, because it is so abstract, is the concept of 'sentence'. It isn't enough to reiterate several times that 'a sentence begins with a capital letter and ends with a full stop' . That doesn't explain to them what 'sentence' means, it only tells them how to mark one. Many of the tasks in this book are designed to help with this concept building.

Learning about grammar gives children the tools to be able to talk about and understand their language development. All words in a sentence can be divided according to their usage into different classes: nouns, verbs, adjectives, adverbs, etc. A word which may ostensibly be the 'same' may have a very different meaning, according to its usage:

The *well* dried up. (noun)
I feel *well* today. (adjective)
The tears *well* in her eyes. (verb)
He plays *well*. (adverb)
Well – who would believe it? (interjection)
Girls, as *well* as boys, play football. (preposition)

(Current non-Standard English also uses the word 'well' in an adjectival capacity, eg 'I was *well* pleased' – but although you can say 'the house was *well*-appointed', which also uses the word in an adjectival capacity, the first example is not good English.)

The concepts of grammar and punctuation are, of course, not the only elements to be considered for good writing skills development. There are times when the concepts need to be taught in isolation and times when they need to be shown as functional, so that children become motivated to learn more about the language because they are inspired by the need to write. Once learned, children will always be able to use their knowledge of parts of speech and punctuation to improve their writing skills.

How to use this book

The activity pages in this book are designed to supplement any English language activities you pursue in the classroom. They are intended to add to your pupils' knowledge of how the English language works.

They can be used with individual children or with small groups, as the need arises. The text on each page has been kept as short as possible so that beginning readers will feel confident to tackle the sheets without too much teacher input, though some children may require you to read through the page carefully with them before they embark upon the activity. The order in which the pages is arranged is not necessarily the order in which children should tackle them. Rather, they should be used randomly as and when reinforcement of a particular need is recognised.

It is not the author's intention that a teacher should expect all children to complete all sheets, and particularly not in any particular period of time. A flexible approach, and a knowledge of the sheets and the children's needs, will provide the teacher with a bank of work that will enable children to extend their knowledge and understanding of the writing process and thus their mastery of it.

Many of the sheets can be modified in simple ways to provide more reinforcement. The 'star' activities are designed as short extension activities which provide a fun element to the worksheet.

Links to the National Curriculum

This book fits in with the National Curriculum programme of study for Key Stage 1 Writing by offering practice in the acquisition of the following key skills:

2   Key Skills

c   In punctuation, pupils should be taught that punctuation is essential to help a reader to understand what is written. Pupils should be given opportunities to read their work aloud in order to understand the connections between the punctuation of a sentence and intonation and emphasis. Pupils should be taught to punctuate their writing, be consistent in their use of capital letters, full stops and question marks, and begin to use commas.

d   In spelling, pupils should be taught to:

- write each letter of the alphabet;

- use their knowledge of sound–symbol relationships and phonological patterns;

- recognise and use simple spelling patterns;

- write common letter strings within familiar and common words;

- spell commonly occurring simple words;

- spell words with common prefixes and suffixes.

Pupils should be taught to check the accuracy of their spelling, and to use word books and dictionaries, identifying initial letters as the means of locating words. They should be given opportunities to experiment with the spelling of complex words and to discuss misapplied generalisations and other reasons for misspellings. Close attention should be paid to word families.

3.   Standard English and Language Study

a   Pupils should be introduced to the vocabulary, grammar and structures of written standard English, including subject–verb agreement, and the use of the verb 'to be' in past and present tenses. They should be taught to apply their existing linguistic knowledge, drawn from oral language and their experience of reading, to develop their understanding of the sentence and how word choice and order are crucial to clarity of meaning. Pupils should be given opportunities to discuss the organisation of more complex texts, and the way sentences link together.

b   Pupils' interest in words and their meanings should be developed, and their vocabulary should be extended through consideration and discussion of words with similar meanings, opposites and words with more than one meaning.

Extension ideas

The following suggestions are for activities which will develop grammatical and punctuation concepts, and good attitudes towards them.

- Make a game out of capital letters and full stops. Ask the children to work on tasks which use, for example, three capital letters and three full stops. Can anybody write something which needs four capital letters and three full stops? Or five capital letters and three full stops?

- Play the 'ing' game. Have the children sitting in a circle and let them come out one by one to demonstrate or mime an 'ing' word – eg running, laughing, ironing, skating. The rest of the children have to guess what they are doing.

- Play the same game with adjectives. Give the demonstrator a card with an adjective on it. The rest of the children choose something for the child to do in the way the adjective asks them to. For example, they might ask the child to 'skip' and the child's card says 'sad' or 'happy'. Be careful which adjectives you choose, but it's very good fun to give, for instance, a colour so that the child has to 'skip' in a 'green' way. This will give the children lots of laugh about – after the laughter, discuss why it can't be done.

- Play a verb and tense game. You say a sentence in the present tense, eg 'we are listening to the radio' and the children have to change it to something you will do tomorrow or did yesterday.

- Write blackboard stories together. Have the children compose the sentences together but as you write the words on the board with the children reading them aloud with you, stop and ask 'when shall we put the full stop?' 'What do we need now for the next word?' 'What do we need for the girl's name?' etc.

- Write out a sentence with a large felt-tip pen and cut the words out. Hand the words out to the children and ask for the word that begins your sentence – 'Who's got "The" with a capital letter?' 'Who's got "rabbit"?' 'Now we need a verb – who's got a verb?' When you get to this bit, remind the children what a verb is. As you collect the words, stick them to the board and have the children read the sentence as you go along.

- Play a 'root' word game. Write a work such as 'cheer' on the board and give the children five minutes to brainstorm all the words they can think of that have 'cheer' in them.

- Children love 'little' words. Teach them all the prepositions. Let them make a list of them as they come across them in their reading.

- Encourage the building of word banks or word dictionaries in any way that you can – they can be used for spelling, for reminding children of different words, as a useful kind of thesaurus. Once the child has written and used a word five times in the right context it can be assumed to be part of her active vocabulary.

Doing words

Words that tell us what someone or something is doing are called verbs.

read

brush

swing

Draw boxes round the verbs in this story.

The alien landed on Earth. He parked his UFO on a

street in town and climbed out. People came to see

what was happening. They thought it was a joke.

Perhaps it was an advert for a new TV programme.

They laughed at the alien. The alien wished he was

back home.

Colour the star if you can write what happened next.

Naming things

Words that name things are called **nouns**.

Colour the pictures. Write the right word in the box.

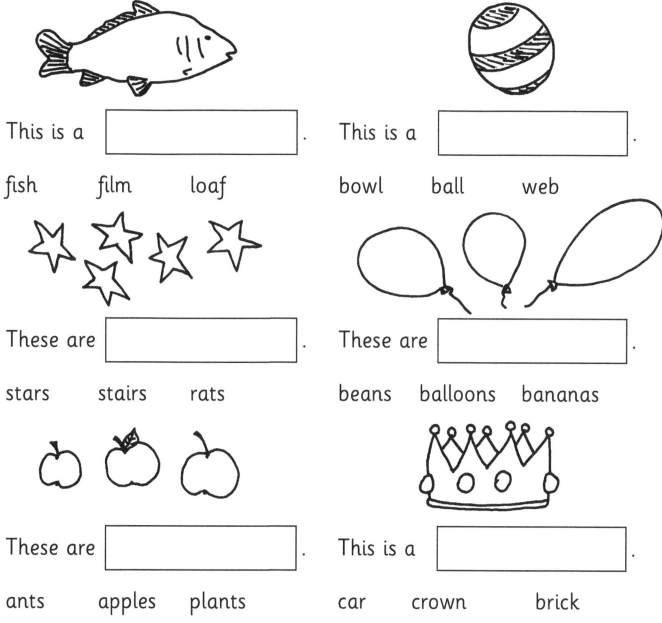

This is a [   ] .

fish   film   loaf

This is a [   ] .

bowl   ball   web

These are [   ] .

stars   stairs   rats

These are [   ] .

beans   balloons   bananas

These are [   ] .

ants   apples   plants

This is a [   ] .

car   crown   brick

Colour the star if
you can read all the
words.

Choose the right word

Words that name things are called **nouns**.

Can you choose the right noun for these pictures? Write a sentence to say what it is:

Is it ...
a moon?
a star?
a planet?

It is _____ .

Is it ...
a bike?
a train?
a car?

It is _____ .

Is it ...
a cat?
a dog?
a fish?

It is _____ .

Is it ...
a bun?
an ice cream?
a banana?

It is _____ .

Is it ...
a fork?
a knife?
a spoon?

It is _____ .

Is it ...
a horse?
a bird?
a butterfly?

It is _____ .

Colour the star if you can make a list of all the nouns.

Word puzzle

All of these words are nouns. Can you work them out?

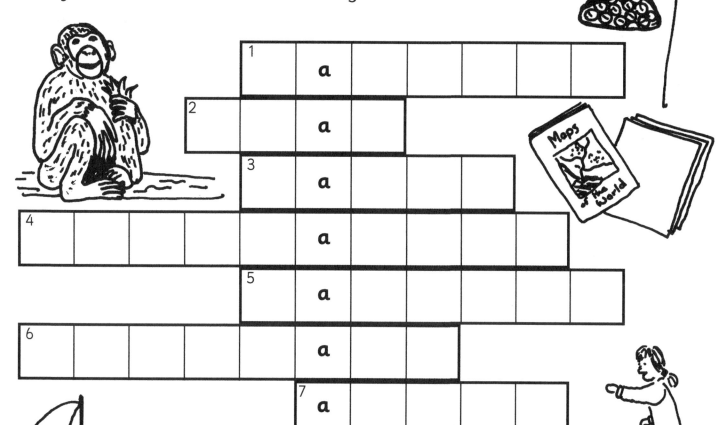

1.   a
2.   a
3.   a
4.   a
5.   a
6.   a
7.   a
8.   a

1   You blow it up.
2   You sail in it.
3   You draw on it.
4   A kind of ape.
5   Small round coloured glass balls.
6   A game you play by kicking.
7   A book of maps.
8   Land surrounded by sea.

Colour the star if you can draw all the nouns.

People's names

People have names. Their names begin with a capital letter. Names are called **Proper nouns**. Write the names of all the children in your class. Don't forget to begin each one with a capital letter.

Colour the star if you can read all the names.

-ing words

How many -ing words do you know?

_____ ing   _____ ing   _____ ing

_____ ing   _____ ing   _____ ing

_____ ing   _____ ing   _____ ing

Colour the star if you can draw three more 'ing' words of your own.

Describing words

Describing words are called **adjectives**. They tell you what something is like.

a **broken** pencil

a **heavy** box

a **long** scarf

Think of four adjectives for each picture.

_____

_____

_____

_____

_____

_____

_____

_____

Colour the star if you can write a poem about one of the pictures.

Describe yourself

Lots of adjectives could be used to describe you. How many can you think of?

kind?   young?   short?   tall?

brown-eyed?   pretty?   clever?   blond-haired?

I am _____

I am _____

I am _____

I am _____

I am _____

I am _____

I am _____

I am _____

Draw a picture of yourself.

If we describe something, we give a 'description'.

Colour the star if you can write a description of your favourite toy.

Making pairs

Here are two sets of words. One set is nouns. One set is adjectives.

Cut out all the words. Work out which adjective goes best with which noun. Stick them side by side on a sheet of paper.

Adjectives	Nouns
fierce	water
wild	armchair
cloudy	grass
comfortable	bird
fast	sky
slow	tiger
green	face
old	snail
dirty	car
shallow	hat

Nouns are naming words.

Adjectives are describing words.

Colour the star if you can draw a picture for each phrase.

Opposites

All these words are adjectives. Draw lines to match the opposites.

heavy	young
old	hot
big	clean
short	deep
cold	fat
dirty	tall
wide	kind
cruel	light
shallow	narrow
thin	small

Write a sentence for each word.

Colour the star if you can make up five more pairs of opposite adjectives of your own.

Get the right order

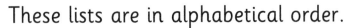

These lists are in alphabetical order.

| ant |
| bear |
| cat |
| donkey |

| ape |
| dog |
| giraffe |
| kangaroo |

This list is not. Cut out the words and stick them in alphabetical order on a sheet of paper.

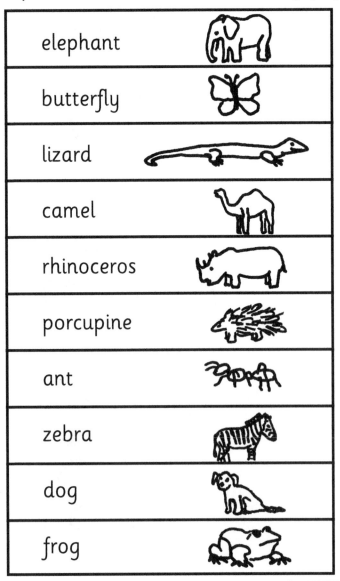

elephant	
butterfly	
lizard	
camel	
rhinoceros	
porcupine	
ant	
zebra	
dog	
frog	

Colour the star if you can draw a picture of an elephant.

Good order

Sometimes when you're putting things in alphabetical order, the words begin with the same letter. When this happens you get the first letters in alphabetical order, and then the second letters.

baby
bend
black
bunch

Write these lists, putting the words in alphabetical order.

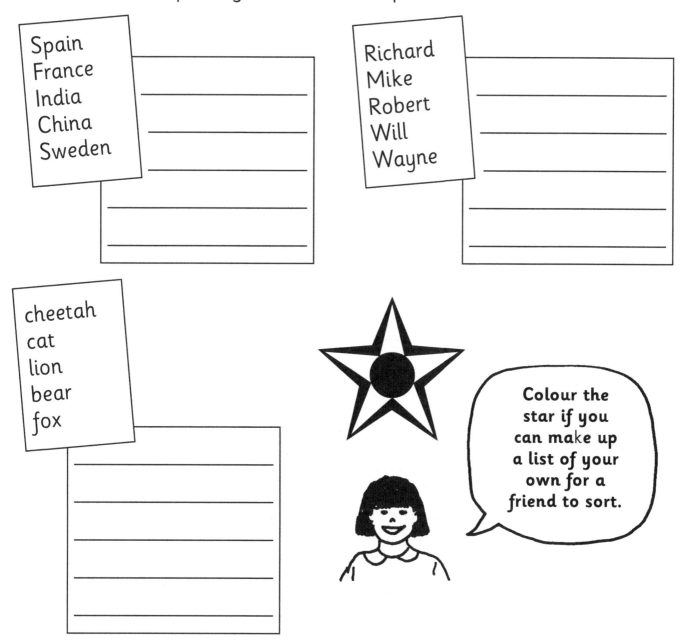

Spain
France
India
China
Sweden

_____
_____
_____
_____
_____

Richard
Mike
Robert
Will
Wayne

_____
_____
_____
_____
_____

cheetah
cat
lion
bear
fox

_____
_____
_____
_____
_____

Colour the star if you can make up a list of your own for a friend to sort.

Thinking of words

Look at the pictures. Make a list of all the words that come in to your head:

Colour the star if you can write a story from one of your word lists.

Missing verbs

Read the sentences. Choose the right words to fill in the spaces.

snowed   went   are going   had

will have   will go   will be

Yesterday we ——————— to the park.

Today we ——————— ——————— swimming.

Next week we ——————— ——————— to the cinema.

When it was my birthday, I ——————— a party.

Next year I hope I ——————— ——————— a new bike.

I made a snowman when it ——————— .

Tomorrow ——————— ——————— Saturday.

Colour the star if you can write another six sentences with verbs.

Think of a word

Think of a word that means the same, or almost the same, as the word in the first column. The first one has been done for you.

friend	**pal**
say	
big	
little	
shop	
wash	
walk	
see	
jump	
finish	
begin	

Colour the star if you can read your words to a friend.

Think of an opposite

Think of a word that means the opposite of:

in

still

quiet

nice

little

many

over

big

down

happy

Colour the star if you can read all your words to a friend.

Beginning sounds

Write three words for each picture, each beginning with the same sound.

big	beautiful	butterfly
_____	_____	_____
_____	_____	_____
_____	_____	_____
_____	_____	_____
_____	_____	_____
_____	_____	_____

Colour the star if you can write another word for each picture.

Sentence sense

Sentences start with capital letters.
They end with full stops.
Sentences make sense.

Cut out these boxes and stick them on a piece of paper to make sensible sentences.

Colour the star if you can copy the sentences.

school every day except Saturday and Sunday.	ride my bike.
I can	We go to
is very kind.	we sing happy songs.
In assembly	My teacher
My dad	We read
lot of books at home.	a new bike for my birthday.
I would like	is a good cook.

Finish the sentence

Can you finish these sentences? Don't forget the full stops!

Birds have wings and —————————————————

Butterflies are —————————————————

Flowers grow in —————————————————

In the rain we —————————————————

We have to —————————————————

My friend is —————————————————

At school we —————————————————

Last week —————————————————

Colour the star if you can draw a butterfly.

Start the sentence

Can you write the start of these sentences? Don't forget to begin with a capital letter.

———————————————— can play football.

———————————————— the ball.

———————————————— under the table.

———————————————— in the park.

———————————————— to bed.

———————————————— in the morning.

———————————————— a blue car.

———————————————— after breakfast.

Colour the star if you can make up four sentences of your own.

Sentences

Write a sentence for each number on the picture of a dog.

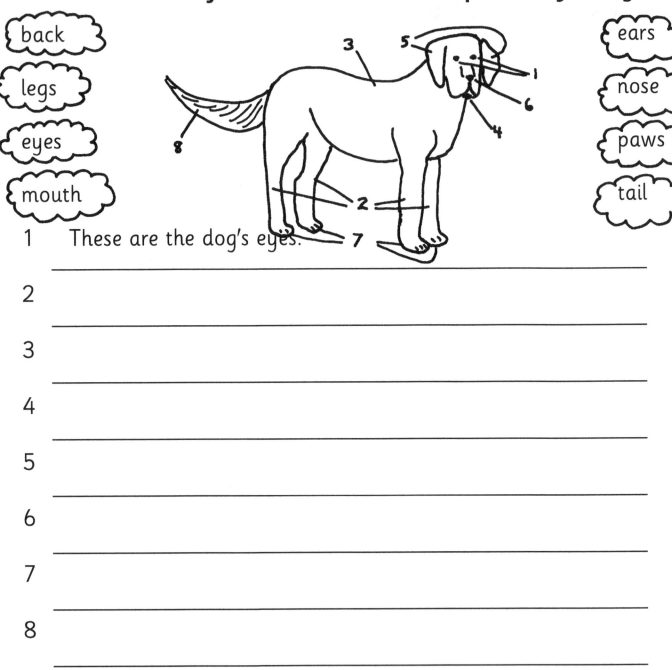

back

legs

eyes

mouth

ears

nose

paws

tail

1   These are the dog's eyes.

2

3

4

5

6

7

8

Colour the star if you can write a poem about the dog.

Capitals and full stops

Can you put the capital letters and full stops in this story?

on friday we went to the safari park it was our

school trip we went on a big coach everybody sat by

their friend we had packed lunches and drinks at the

safari park we saw lots of wild animals the monkeys

climbed on to the coach and made us laugh

Colour the star if you can write a monkey story.

What's wrong?

Look at the picture. There are ten things wrong with it.
What are they?

1 _____

2 _____

3 _____

4 _____

5 _____

6 _____

7 _____

8 _____

9 _____

10 _____

Colour the star if you can tell a friend what's wrong.

Right order

Here are six sentences. Cut them out and stick the words in the right order so that the sentences make sense.

right. Colour if you this star can the put sentence

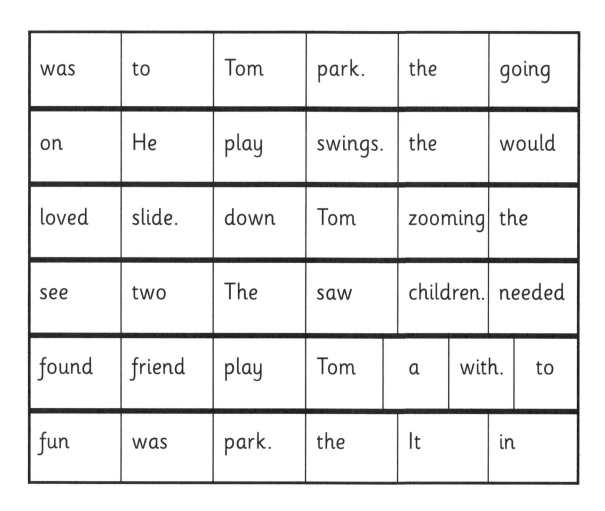

was	to	Tom	park.	the	going
on	He	play	swings.	the	would
loved	slide.	down	Tom	zooming	the
see	two	The	saw	children.	needed
found	friend	play	Tom	a	with.	to
fun	was	park.	the	It	in

Secret code

1	2	3	4	5	6	7	8	9	10	11	12	13
a	b	c	d	e	f	g	h	i	j	k	l	m

14	15	16	17	18	19	20	21	22	23	24	25	26
n	o	p	q	r	s	t	u	v	w	x	y	z

This message is in secret code. Write what it says underneath.

3	1	14		25	15	21		23	18	9	20	5

1		13	5	19	19	1	7	5		9	14	

3	15	4	5	?

Make up your own message here:

Write it in code here:

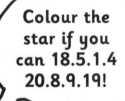

Colour the star if you can 18.5.1.4 20.8.9.19!

Missing words

Can you write in the missing words?

tall   taller   tallest

short   shortest

high   higher

wide

                                                biggest

Colour the star if you can finish:

good   better   _____

Gingerbread man

When the old lady made the Gingerbread man, she:

Cut out the boxes and put the pictures in the right order.
Write a sentence for each one.

1 _____

2 _____

3 _____

4 _____

5 _____

6 _____

7 _____

8 _____

9 _____

Colour the star if you know what happened next.

In the box

Cut out the words and stick them in the right box.

nouns

adjectives

verbs

Colour the star if you can write a story using some of these words.

cat	elephant	walked	ran
dog	brown	tabby	jumped
leaped	big	carton	huge
tree	man	umbrella	ladder
frighten	squeaked	whisker	tail
knew	small	tiny	grey

In the circle

Cut out the words and stick them in the right circle.

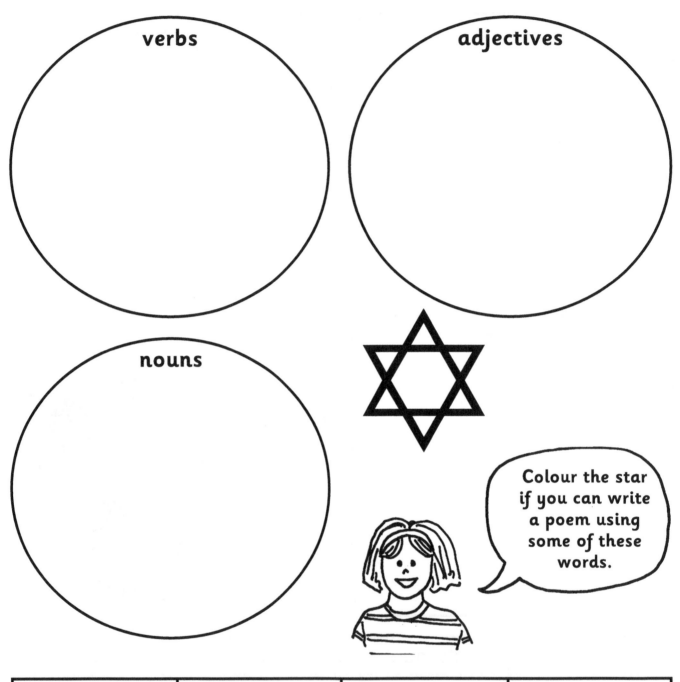

verbs

adjectives

nouns

Colour the star if you can write a poem using some of these words.

night	black	said	midnight
sky	star	twinkling	made
blue	high	moon	silver
wanted	had	kind	gave
lit	went	sun	shining

Lots of lists

Commas have many different uses. They are used in lists. When there is a list of words used in a sentence, each word is separated from the next one by a comma.

> We need a chair, a table and some cups.
>
> Mrs Green was a nice, friendly and kind teacher.
>
> The alien stopped, stared, screamed and then ran away.

The last word on the list is usually joined by 'and' instead of a comma.

Can you put commas in these sentences?

The monster was huge ugly and spiky.

The alien's eye was glittering gleaming and very big.

Everybody trembled shook and shivered with fear.

Write three sentences of your own.

Colour the star if you can write a story about an alien coming to school.

Capital letters

Capital letters should always be used for:

beginning sentences
Write a sentence here:

---

people's names
Write three names here:

1

2

3

---

names of places
Write three place names here:

1

2

3

---

names of streets and roads
Write three road names here:

1

2

3

---

days of the week
Write three names of days here:

1

2

3

---

months of the year
Write three names of months here:

1

2

3

Colour the star if you can write all the months of the year.

Don't forget the capital letter

People's names are nouns. They are special because they belong to someone. To show they are special they begin with a capital letter. They are called **Proper Nouns**.

 Tom  Anna  Jack  Ravinder

Can you begin these Proper Nouns?

——en   (a boy's name)   ——ohn   (a boy's name)

——racy   (a girl's name)   ——mma   (a girl's name)

Mrs ——reen   (a lady's name)   Mr —— rown   (a man's name)

These people words don't have capital letters. Can you fill in the spaces?

——an   ——ady   ——irl

——oy   ——eople   ——en

——adies   ——irls   ——oys

Colour the star if you can make a list of Proper Nouns beginning with each letter of the alphabet.

Places have names

Places have names. Their names are Proper Nouns so they begin with a capital letter.

Do you know the names of these countries?

——ngland   ——hina   ——pain

——ales   ——cotland   ——reland

——rance   ——reece   ——ermany

Do you know the names of these cities?

——ondon   ——lasgow   ——ew —— ork

——aris   ——ome   ——ardiff

——elhi   ——xeter   ——irmingham

Do you know the names of these places?

——iverpool   ——anchester   ——irmingham

——hester   ——over   ——ornwall

Colour the star if you can put all the place names in alphabetial order.

Surprise! surprise!

Exclamation marks are there to show you how to read the sentence.
They show some kind of surprise.

Read these sentences.

> The girl had three dogs with her.
>
> The girl had three dogs with her!

What happens when you put an exclamation mark on the end of
these sentences?

Ouch

Don't do it

Stand up straight

What a lovely day

Stop

Silly me

Write six sentences of your own with exclamation marks.

1 _____

2 _____

3 _____

4 _____

5 _____

6 _____

**Colour the star
if you can swap
your sentences
with a friend and
read them aloud.**

Questions, questions

Q How do you know a sentence is a question?

B Because it asks something and it ends with '?'.

Look at the picture. Write some questions about it here:

Who _____

What _____

Where _____

When _____

Why _____

How _____

Colour the star if you can swap with a friend and answer each other's questions.

Question quiz

Put question marks on the end of the sentences that are questions and full stops on those that are not.

Where is the teddy bear

Is it very old

She wonders where the teddy is

How long has she had it

She says it's older than her

She thinks it's very special

It is a big bear, isn't it

It growls

Can teddy bears speak

Does she think it talks

It's a very special bear

Is it a special bear

Colour the star if you can write the story of 'A special bear goes to town'.

Get the right order

Cut the words out and stick them in the right order to make a story.

There	boy	Jack.
He	big	was
and	a	fishing
once	it	went
caught	for	fish.
His	a	called
mum	cooked	lunch.

Colour the star if you can finish the story.

The alphabet

Join the alphabet dots to make the picture. Start at 'a'.

Write the alphabet in capital letters here. Make sure you get the letters in the right order.

A _ _ _ _ _ _ _ _ _ _ _ _ _

_ _ _ _ _ _ _ _ _ _ _ _ _

Colour the star if you can say the alphabet aloud with a friend.

Noun wordsearch

Look for eight nouns in the wordsearch.

m	o	n	s	t	e	r	m
a	s	p	a	c	e	r	o
l	e	a	r	t	h	r	p
i	p	z	y	q	j	o	l
e	s	t	a	r	m	c	a
n	b	c	w	n	f	k	n
a	z	k	j	g	x	e	e
z	m	o	o	n	e	t	t

The words can go across or down.

List the words here:

Colour the star if you
can write a poem
using the words.

Adjective wordserach

Look for eight adjectives in the wordsearch.

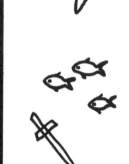

w	l	d	s	a	n	d	y
i	c	w	n	j	o	x	m
g	w	e	o	b	l	f	u
g	p	t	q	g	d	i	k
l	w	r	e	c	k	e	d
y	u	v	g	r	e	e	n
t	b	l	u	e	j	z	y
p	r	e	c	i	o	u	s

The words can go across or down.

List the words here:

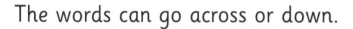

Colour the star is you can write a poem using the words.

Verb wordsearch

Look for eight verbs in the wordsearch.

w	l	s	o	w	e	d	p
a	g	m	n	d	u	g	l
t	r	k	l	y	z	b	a
e	e	s	h	o	n	e	n
r	w	c	v	s	z	u	t
e	j	u	w	x	c	t	e
d	p	i	c	k	e	d	d
f	l	o	w	e	r	e	d

The words can go across or down.

List the words here:

Colour the star if you can write a story using the words.

CPSIA information can be obtained at www.ICGtesting.com
Printed in the USA
LVOW02s1143061114

3754LVUK00006B/11/P